PHYLLIS SECKLER
(SOROR MERAL)

COLLECTED POEMS
1946-1996

PHYLLIS SECKLER (SOROR MERAL)

COLLECTED POEMS
1946-1996

EDITED BY

DAVID SHOEMAKER

& LAUREN GARDNER

Published in 2017 by

Temple of the Silver Star
P.O. Box 215483
Sacramento, California 95821, USA

Founded in Service to the A∴A∴

totss.org

ISBN: 0-9976686-6-0
ISBN-13: 978-0-9976686-6-7

TABLE OF CONTENTS

For Soror Meral

INTRODUCTION

Do what thou wilt shall be the whole of the Law.

Poetry is one of the most intimate expressions of the human soul. In editing these writings, I had the sense of getting to know Soror Meral in a very personal way, seeing glimpses of her inner world across several different periods of her life. Of course, the continuity of her voice, and the intensity of her aspiration, remained consistent throughout all of them. I was very struck too by the simplicity and childlike quality of these poems. Also, it seems that she felt everything so very deeply. In a way, this has been a helpful reminder of how sensitivity can itself be a strength, and not a liability as often imagined.

Her attunement to the natural world in these poems also moved me, and several poems brought me back to a time in my childhood when I felt particularly immersed in natural cycles. Most of all, in how she wrote about tending her garden, I glimpsed the way she must have approached nurturing others that she cared about. To me, this is a reminder that Thelema, at the beginning and end of the day, is about love.

Lauren Gardner
Spring 2017 e.v.

In my time knowing and working with Soror Meral — roughly the last decade of her life — it became abundantly clear that her poetry and her art were among the most deeply personal expressions of her unique genius. While her practical knowledge of magick and mysticism, earned through decades of diligent personal work and teaching, was at the core of her instructional writings, it is in her poetry and art that we glimpse the beating heart of her aspiration and devotion to the Great Work. In the poems presented here, we see Soror Meral's passion for life and love, her incessant quest for deepening intimacy with her Holy Guardian Angel and Nuit, and her belief in the transformational power of the spiritual path of Thelema.

Soror Meral was always ready, even eager, to be instructed by life itself. Echoing the sentiments expressed by my co-editor above, she offered these thoughts in her autobiographical writings:

> Being in love sparked the beginning of my poetry. It is often the case with me that love has sparked an outpouring of inspiration on poetic lines. In later years I was to understand even more deeply what I had known ever since the days when I lived at Winona Blvd. [...] It is that we humans are here on earth to learn how to love. This is the law of the Universe. Much later I learned how intense and how pure the love of the Holy Guardian Angel was for his partner or child. We must learn to return this love [...] every time we humans love someone or something. The love might be for family, children, friends, nature, our work, or a partner. It is all a lesson of great importance.

It is our hope that the poems presented here kindle the flame of aspiration in your hearts, encouraging you along the path of your own Great Work. May you each come to know and to express this divine love in all your thoughts, words and deeds.

Love is the law, love under will.

David Shoemaker
Summer 2017 e.v.
Anno Legis V[iii]

BIOGRAPHICAL SKETCH[1]

Phyllis Evelina Seckler (neé Pratt, also known as Soror Meral) was born on June 18, 1917, in Edmonton, Alberta. She was the second child of Bickerton Pratt of Roughton, Wales, and Dorothy Leake of Massachusetts. The family later moved to Victoria, British Columbia, then to Seattle, and finally to various locations in Southern California. Seckler graduated from George Washington High School in Los Angeles in 1935, and soon after enrolled in Los Angeles City College, where she studied drama and art.

After a rift with her mother, Phyllis moved out of the family home and began working to support herself while attending night classes in drama at City College. This proved to be a fateful choice, as it was at these classes that she became acquainted with her future husband Paul Seckler, as well as Regina Kahl, her drama teacher. Kahl was, of course, the presiding Priestess at the Gnostic Masses being presented at Agape Lodge, the primary outpost of Ordo Templi Orientis (O.T.O.) in the United States. Agape Lodge was the epicenter of Thelema outside of Aleister Crowley's headquarters in England, and Seckler was entranced by the intellectuals and free-thinkers she found there. She wrote of her first visit:

> As I was leaving, a short person, older, but looking quite knowledgeable, asked if I knew about Aleister Crowley. Of course I had never heard of him, and in those days, who had? But Wilfred Smith then proceeded to recite some verses of Crowley's, and I was duly impressed. As I walked down the street, I thought to myself that I had to get to know these people better, for I was really starved for intellectual stimulus.

---

[1] Adapted from the original version published in Seckler, *The Thoth Tarot, Astrology & Other Selected Writings.* (Sacramento: Temple of the Silver Star 2017). All quoted passages are from Seckler's unpublished autobiographical writings.

Seckler began attending Gnostic Masses regularly, and soon was able to rent a room for herself in the Lodge (1746 Winona Boulevard in Los Angeles) and participate more actively in the life of its residents, including Jane Wolfe. Wolfe was the only member of the California O.T.O. to have met and worked directly with Crowley himself, and as such Crowley depended on her to convey the teachings she had received from him at the Abbey of Thelema in Cefalu, Sicily. The importance of Wolfe's influence on Seckler's life cannot be overstated.

Seckler worked as a housekeeper in the Lodge to help pay the rent, and she delighted in the Thelemic culture and fraternity she found there. She wrote of these years:

> Wilfred was prevailed upon to discuss the meaning of the Mass after the performance, and then after that we sat around and discussed various matters. Often, we would ask Wilfred to throw the Yi King sticks for various persons in the group. Sometimes he had to get an answer for everyone in the room.
>
> Regina was very good at putting parties together, and often after the Mass we had refreshments and a party-like atmosphere, but with an intellectual emphasis. Jane Wolfe often sat in a wing chair on the opposite side of the fireplace from the seat which Wilfred always took, but she would often doze off, for she had heard Wilfred say the same things so very many times. Sometimes the older people would retire, and we young people were left to sit around the fire in the winter and talk amongst ourselves.

Paul and Phyllis Seckler were married in the summer of 1938. Soon after, Paul moved to the Midwest, leaving Phyllis temporarily on her own. Seckler's occult interests continued, however, and she took her Minerval and First degrees in O.T.O. in 1939. After continued informal mentoring from Jane Wolfe, Seckler was admitted as a Probationer of A∴A∴ under Wolfe in June of 1940. She also began studying astrology with Frederick Mellinger, whose teachings formed the foundation of Seckler's approach to this subject for the remainder of her life. Meanwhile,

Paul Seckler had returned to Los Angeles. Phyllis forgave him for his absence, and they resumed their relationship.

Agape Lodge found a new home at 1003 Orange Grove in Pasadena in 1942. The Secklers were among its founding residents, along with Mellinger, Smith, Wolfe, Kahl, Joe and Grace Miller, Jack Parsons, and his partner Betty Northrup (the younger sister of Parsons' wife, Helen) and others. This arrangement was intermittent, however, due to the family's turbulent financial state. Seckler's journals also show her annoyance at the inconsiderateness of some of the Lodge's residents.

Grady McMurtry and Karl Germer visited Agape Lodge during the mid-1940s, and Seckler's relationships with these men would be of great importance for the rest of her life. Working hard to support her family and continue her education, Seckler remained as active in O.T.O. as she could, given the constraints on her time and money. Her situation improved temporarily when Parsons resigned and Roy Leffingwell took over the leadership of Agape Lodge. Leffingwell helped Seckler by offering her rides to and from Lodge events, and eventually a romance developed. She wrote:

> Now began an affair which was to last only for three years.
> But I have always considered Roy to be the greatest love of
> my life. Being in love sparked the beginning of my poetry.

This affair ended in 1949 when Leffingwell suffered a stroke and his family barred Seckler from further contact with him. In the meantime (1947), Crowley had died, and Germer took over as head of O.T.O. and A∴A∴. A strong bond of friendship developed between Seckler and her primary Thelemic teachers, Germer and Wolfe. Their extensive correspondence spanned many years, and the most important of these letters are presented in *Karl Germer: Selected Letters 1928-1962*.[2]

---

[2] Published in 2017 by the Temple of the Silver Star.

As Agape Lodge sputtered and finally died in the 1950s, Seckler, Germer, and Wolfe continued their work, with Seckler performing extensive typing and editing of Crowley materials for Germer, and Wolfe directly supervising Seckler's work in A∴A∴. In the meantime, Seckler had finally separated from her husband, finished a Master's degree in art at UCLA, and began work as a high school art teacher in Livermore, California. Seckler's correspondence with Germer during these years was particularly important, as it was in these letters that he confirmed Seckler's status as an Adeptus Minor 5°=6□ of A∴A∴. Also importantly, Germer's instruction on the nature of the Holy Guardian Angel became the foundation of Seckler's understanding and exploration of the subject — in addition to her own direct experiences, of course — to the great benefit of her students. Further, Germer had conferred the IXth degree of O.T.O. to Seckler, including instruction in the Order's central mysteries.

Seckler's relationship with Germer included some romantic elements, at least intermittently. She wrote the following in regard to a driving trip she took with Germer in 1955:

> Karl drove me up the mountain, as he wanted to see the redwoods there. We got out of the car and stood under a very large tree, and there Karl told me that he loved me. I was not of the same mind exactly, but admired Karl and liked him a lot. I was also very cognizant of the fact that he and I had a great deal in common through our spiritual experiences. Further, some years previous, perhaps in 1952, my inner voice had told me that I must be a partner for Karl.

As Seckler's magical relationship with Germer continued, so did her time as Jane Wolfe's A∴A∴ student come to end —Wolfe died in 1958 after several years of declining health. Meanwhile, Seckler had remarried and moved into her new husband's home in San Jose, California. She continued corresponding extensively with Germer, meeting him in person whenever possible, until his death in 1962 from prostate cancer. Germer's death set the stage for a long period of silence and (relative) stagnation in the

Thelemic world. O.T.O. was inactive, and the group of California Thelemites had long since been fragmented. After divorcing her second husband in 1963, Seckler devoted herself to raising her family and continuing her teaching career— while also developing her painting, writing poetry, and carrying on extensive correspondence with the remaining adherents of Thelema. These included Marjorie Cameron, Israel Regardie, Gerald Yorke and, last but certainly not least, Grady McMurtry.

Seckler and McMurtry had corresponded intermittently for many years, but their correspondence became more frequent in 1968, following the theft of Crowley's magical implements, robes, and private notebooks from Sascha Germer's home. Seckler invested a large amount of time over the next few years investigating this incident, with mixed results. Meanwhile, Seckler invited McMurtry to come to California, at her expense, so that they might work together to reactivate the O.T.O.. (McMurtry had received authorization from Crowley to take such steps, should Germer fail to make adequate provisions for a successor.) Seckler, McMurtry and Mildred Burlingame (a former member of Agape Lodge) officially reinaugurated the O.T.O. in July of 1969, and McMurtry performed his first O.T.O. initiations soon after, in a park near the Russian River.

Over the ensuing several years, Seckler became increasingly disillusioned with McMurtry's growing alcohol and drug use, and the erratic behavior it created. She was also supporting him financially, as he was too ill to find or keep employment. She had admitted him to A∴A∴ as her Probationer in 1970, but later expelled him after becoming frustrated with his failure to do the work required to progress to Neophyte. McMurtry's condition improved temporarily after he attempted suicide and underwent psychiatric treatment at Napa State Hospital. After he returned home, the work of reconstituting the O.T.O. continued. Seckler wrote:

> We performed a very few initiations, mostly Minervals. Most of these people never went on to First Degree. I really think

they had some sort of over-blown expectations about the O.T.O. due to Crowley's writings. Also they had an idea about the glamour of occult studies. They weren't prepared for a tiny pioneering effort, nor were they about to do much work for themselves or for the O.T.O. as it then was. Further, Crowley's writings were difficult to obtain and ignorance about Thelema was widespread. It was this marked ignorance that made me resolve to write and publish.

And publish she did. Beginning in 1973, and for nearly twenty-five years thereafter, Seckler published the journal *In the Continuum* (I.T.C.) under the aegis of her newly formed College of Thelema (C.O.T.). She envisioned the College as a much-needed source of preparatory instruction for aspirants to A∴A∴ having seen too many students fail due to a lack of such preparation. She also continued her initiatory and instructional work within A∴A∴ itself, having been the most senior member at the time of Germer's death. As this work continued, her relationship with McMurtry finally came to an end. The couple separated in 1975, the same year Seckler retired from her many years of professional teaching. Accordingly, she was now free to devote herself fully to occult study and teaching. She presided over and assisted with many O.T.O. initiations in the following years, including the initiations of many of the luminaries of the next generation of Thelemites. She possessed a deep love for the Gnostic Mass, instructing her students in the Mass as she had seen it performed during her time at Agape Lodge. In spite of their turbulent relationship, Seckler and McMurtry continued to work together sporadically, if not harmoniously, until his death in 1985. In the meantime, Seckler had been granted a charter for 418 Lodge of O.T.O., and she continued her tireless work publishing *I.T.C.* and teaching a small cadre of personal students at her new home in Oroville, California.

It was through C.O.T. that Seckler came into contact with the co-editor of this present volume, David Shoemaker. In 2000, Seckler granted a charter to Shoemaker, authorizing him to continue the work of A∴A∴ and C.O.T. independently, should the need arise. Over the last few years of her life, she revised her Last

Will in recognition of Shoemaker's charter, laying the foundation for the emergence of the autonomous organization now known as the Temple of the Silver Star.

Seckler remained an influential force in O.T.O. throughout these years, although she had for the most part retired from performing initiations or serving in formal governing roles. She retained the Mastership of 418 Lodge until April 2004, when she passed the Master's chair to Shoemaker. Just over a month later, on May 31, 2004, she died peacefully, surrounded by loved ones, as the Holy Books of Thelema were read at her bedside.

COLLECTED POEMS

SACRIFICE

Lord, accept this offering I make,
This life, this heart and soul and mind.
I endure, only for Thee to awake,
Waiting for Thy ties of Love to bind
Me, to take my will and hammer it
Into a spear for Thine own use;
To take my joy and fashion it
Into a cup, Thy force to house;
To take my labour and transmute it
Into an echo of Thy name:
O let Thy Presence fill and enlighten me
That I might cry aloud with Thy Flame.

Chain me to Thy Will, Lord of Divine Liberty;
Burn me with Thy Fire, Lord of Everlasting Desire;
Consume me, fill me with Thy Sun of Beauty;
Enflame me, name me with Thy Wanton Ire.
Ravish me away to Thy Ruby Abode,
This mortal shell, Thine emerald wings enfold.
Until my will becomes Thine, O Master Soul of Mine
And my ecstasy is ever Thy lovely cup of wine;
My joy, Thy joy to see for all eternity,
My desire and Thine moving to seal our Affinity.

Thy spirit enflames mine in prayer;
Thy unearthly music strikes to my core;
My effort is gone, whirled away in the roar
Of soul shattering bliss, I am dissolved in Thy kiss.
I am the fulfillment of Thy Will.
I am the vehicle of Thy Love.
I am the Power to show Thy Might,
The Word of enlightenment from above.
I am Thy innermost core, revolving Light
Of Life. I am thine, Thou art mine.
We are One, we are None, we are still.

1946

FLIGHT OF THE SWAN

Slowly circling, slowly whirling,
Slowly the aeons revolve.
Bright winging, brightly singing,
Brightly the swan evolves.

Faintly dying, faintly sighing,
The Being that is I dissolves
Into being, into seeing,
The swan that dips and dives.

Forever reeling, forever wheeling,
Forever the cycles revive
Of the daylight and the darkness,
Of the deaths and lives.

Always turning, always burning,
The shadow and light derives
From the dissolving, always evolving,
Swan-soul that always survives.

1946

A CALL

Adonai!
Admit this storm tossed mortal,
Do you not hear the beating of the hands
Upon Thy gem-starred portal?

Loosen the bands
Of earth, transmute the agony infernal
Into the journey far onto the strands
Of honeyed bliss, of peace eternal.

Adonai! Heed my call!
Let me be touched by Thy angelic kiss
By my energy's renewal and transferal,
Oh, take me unto Thee beyond the Abyss.

1946

LIBERTY

Beloved, I am thy servant,
Adoring, kneeling, stretched suppliant,
Lord of my Soul, Eternal One.
Wrap me, surround me, with Light of thy Sun.

My flame leaps higher, aspirant
To thy Kingdom, I an applicant
To be thy slave, expression of true liberty
Is this, Lord of lustrous limpidity.

I am thy servant and thy queen,
Adored of me, adoring One,
Thou art my lawful King, supreme
Among the eternal Gods and men.

In serving Thee lies my freedom,
Single-purposed I stride along.
Enkindled, enlightened with thy wisdom,
On my lips, and in my heart lies thy song.

Burning and flaming with Thee am I filled,
Body, spirit, and soul entwined
With the Snake of thy Light, my mind
Struck by thy knife, I am stilled.

1946

7

THE UNCONSCIOUS

Hag ridden far down the night
Far into the past stretches the dark
Dancing daughters of desire, the witch,
The ghost, the filmy goblin stomping,
The misshapen shapes of man's false
Beginnings and strivings.

Now ringing around the upright stone
Magically turned to Pan, a bone
Cutting the beasts to see the cruelty run
In flames of blood, hate flaming,
Now demon haunted, twisting, turning,
Overwhelming himself, stumbling
And running in darkest night.
The moon glares in dreadful magic light
Throughout his dreams, an ache of dread.
Whence, oh whither does it all lead?

O'erwhelmed by ghosts of the unconscious,
Dreadful leering faces, he waits in terror
For the phantoms of the dark, fallacious
Reason scarce lifting the shades more.
Running, running down the mists of time.
Will it never end? Murder! The papers scream
And yet another wretch must swing
Unexpurgated of his phantoms and his dreams.

And yet these phantoms of his dark desires
Are his, none other's. His to face the fire
With an Excalibur grasped from out the mire!

Undated

THE VOICE OF GOD

A God came down and spoke to me,
Whilst the darkness wrapped me tenderly,
    A God ope'd His eye and spoke.

A God caught me up in His embrace,
A God showed to me His face,
    A God whom I invoked.

I lived a night enraptured,
The self of me was captured,
    And bended to His yoke.

I loved Him through eternity,
 Wrapped in His God-like amity,
    loved Him e'er I woke.

Broke the dawning soft and clear,
From my eye there slid a tear,
    Alas! my lover spoke.

               1947

NEOPHYTE

Ah, my Lord and Master, I kneel at thy feet,
By arms upflung, breast's passionate beat,
I affirm my passion wildly upsurging
Enflamed and caught by Thee in our merging.

Infinitely tender Thy wings enfold me,
Infinitely tender the words you speak:
Beyond ourselves I know you hold me
Close to thy heart, a part of its beat.

Thy Light sings through me, iridescent
Soul of song, beating rhythm reminiscent
Of light's swift thrust and flight
Through the soul of the adoring neophyte.

1947

SONG TO PAN

Immortal One, immutable,
   God inscrutable,
Immolate with head unbowed
   To Thee am I vowed.

O Thou, with the name of Pan,
   Master of life's swift beat,
O Thou in the guise of a man,
   I moan, I swoon at Thy feet.

Curved hill and hollow rings
   To the tones of Thy pipe;
My, soul in rapture sings,
   I am ready and ripe.

O, glorious goat-like God,
   Paens of praise to Thy name,
Inspired by the force of Thy rod,
   The echoing cry of Thy fame.

I tremble as a leaf before the might
   Of the force of Thy wrath,
Blown before Thee as the flight
   Of the swan in the blast.

O, God of the forest and hills
As we bend we slaken
Our thirst at the rocky rills,
On immortal liquor drunken.

Bedecked and garlanded with roses
On Thy altar I stand;
The rite of our loving discloses
The might of Thy hand.

Ah! I am drained of life's blood,
Lying stripped of emotion,
Whirled away in the flood
Of love's turbulent ocean.

Insatiable God, immutable,
Thou inscrutable,
Immolate with head unbowed,
To Thee am I vowed.

1947

CREATION (I)

There aches a formless void of nothing
    Potentialities in reserve,
Uncreated, unmanifest, woman's loving
    Abyss of reason's curve.

Nothing throbs in loneliness and sorrow,
    Revolving in the empty spaces;
Waiting for the Lord of Life to follow
    Her beckoning, many-wiled faces.

"Come unto me," always she cries,
    Enfolding him in her desire;
Lust for fulfillment in her sighs,
    Her longing lighting his inner fire.

Leaps the flame of his Being,
    Mysterious and wonderful the Way
Of the all-begetting, all-devouring
    Wanderer seeking his lust to allay.

Thus the worlds become created
    In the never-ending dance
Of He, the go'er, Her, the followed;
    Their loves are life's continuance.

1947

QUESTION

Who am I? The wandering soul of me cries,
 In what profound depths the world of me lies;
From what abyss of time and to what eternity
Shall I return, shall I arrive, when I die?

Is there peace, is there hope beyond the grave?
Does the soul struggle in torment or does Lethe lave
The tears and sorrows of life in waters divine,
Losing all but memory in the engulfing waves?

1947

VICTORY

Victory is ours, beloved,
We have won the golden laurels,
We have reaped joy from the sorrows,
    We have won by right.

Victory is ours, beloved,
We have reaped the harvest,
Earned the languorous rest
    Won to the inner sight.

Victory is ours, beloved,
Not as two but as one,
In the royal race we run,
    We have won the Light.

Triumph is ours, beloved,
With footsteps ringing wild
We gave birth to the child,
    Who sprang free of the night.

We saw the child, beloved,
Leap free from the ruins,
From our living effort hewn,
    We saw him triumph over might.

Triumph through love, beloved,
He holds the torch on high,
He shouts freedom to the sky,
    He calls liberty from the height.

From the Light he calls, beloved,
"Brothers waken and live,
Spread the liberty of love,
    Awaken to the Light."

We have won, beloved,
The clarion call has sounded;
Rings through the air around us,
    His words, "Do what thou wilt."

1947

ANSWER

I walked in the valley of shadow
  I walked all alone.
Many the doubts that beset me,
  Many the hideous groan
Of the wind of thoughts o'erwhelming,
  Of the intellect's sand,
That sought to engulf my faint candle
  That I held in my hand.

My one light, my one guide was failing,
  My only path too faint;
On what could I depend for guidance?
  Loud grew my plaint
As I searched in vain for the path before me,
  Searched the sifting sands
And looked long for the way to Adonai,
  Looked long through the Lands,

I forgot the message my heart had to give,
  Forgot its quiet sigh,
"Look up, look up, the light is before you,
  A brilliant star in the sky.
Look not to the earth of change and tomorrow,
  Look not to thoughts and tears,
Ask not why, nor question ever,
  Ask not how of the years.

There is only one path, one light
    One star to follow
One God in heaven and on earth,
    One answer to sorrow.
No thought has realized yet,
    No eyes have seen,
Nor ears have heard, nor touch
    No one has been
Where dwelleth the answer to your life,
    Where is only one law,
The law to love, to give of self entirely,
    To the Lover you never saw."

1948

A WORD OF ADVICE TO MY SPIRIT

Bend before the wind, O spirit frail,
> Bend before it.
Don't try to hold up thy head through the gale,
> Bend before it.
Don't try to stem the tide of emotions wild,
> Bend before them.
Bow your sorrowful head to earth as a child,
> Bend it low.
Lest in resisting the impetuous stir of life
> And bend not low,
Thou find thyself sadly torn by the strife
> And bend no more.

1949

DEPARTURE

Weep you now? But she has gone
    Down the mist of years.

Mourn not her parting, for the sun
    Has dried all her tears.

See the aura of radiance around her
    Wrapping her with her dreams.

See, her dreams have at last found her,
    She is not what she seems.

Look well and see around her shining
    Faith, Hope and Trust, her dreams:

Winging beside her the Spirit of Giving
    Protects her with its beams.

Weep you now for lack of her?
    For her love that was fair?

Weep not now in back of her
    For she has wandered there.

Weep you then that her spirit was so frail?
    Ah, she has her life now in another world.

A world where her giving does not fail,
      Where love's rose petals lie all unfurled.

Weep you for her? Ah, but look,
      There is a woman in her place.

The child has taken all she brought.
      The woman hides her face.

1949

WHAT IS LOVE?

What is love?
Love is faith in the dark
Life that stirs in the womb of time;
Union across the stark
And ancient terrors of the mind.

What is love?
Love is cohesion sought;
Love union on every plane
Beyond emotion and thought
In coldest ice and ardent flame.

What is love?
Love is sacrifice of Self,
A soul-felt urge for immolation;
Love is death and rebirth
Into a god-like transformation.

What is love?
Love is purifying fire,
Burning spirit in the crucible of life,
Spaceless and timeless desire
Creating creation's husband and wife.

What is love?

Love is homage rendered,

Our speech with God who is the end

And goal of Self surrendered,

The Will of the Soul unpenned.

What is love?

Love is the only Law

To govern earthly and heavenly ways:

The sole reason for the flaw

Of division that melts in union's bright blaze.

1949

THE VOICE OF ADONAI

Thy small voice whispers, Oh, Adonai,
    The quiet voice of silence
Whispering my name, my Adonai,
    And holds in abeyance
The material blame; transcending the mind
Of mundane caution, descending to blind
    My earthly sight.

Thy soft voice thunders, oh, Adonai,
    Storming self and bending my way
To Thy pure Truth, my Adonai,
    And Thy Word lives through all of day
And I carry Thy Will in my captured heart
As I wend my steps to my higher part,
    My brightest light.

Thy voice rings through me, Oh, Adonai,
    And sings of our greatest joy;
Thy voice thrilling me, my Adonai;
    Pure gold showers sans alloy,
Shimmering brilliance of Voice of Gold,
Showering down whate'er I may hold
    From ethereal height.

I hear inwards Thy Voice, Oh, Adonai,
      Bidding me listen and follow,
Voice of the Sun and Moon transcendent, my Adonai,
      As kneeling before Thee I vow
To drink at Thy Fount of Inspiration,
To follow Thy Voice of Intuition
      In my dark night.

1949

PLATO'S CAVE

Man lives in a cave of self-inflicted horrors
Whispering of cruelty and torture and pain.
All creatures of the shadow's dark forces
Mumbling in darkness, themselves arraign
Through the black pit of themselves,
Snarling at others, fighting blindly
In selfish greed of ego. Oh, man, but delve
Into thy deepest motives, what do you see?

Do you not comprehend that all of mankind
Is one body? That every blow dealt
Is a blow to yourself? Can you not find
The source of humanity, a certain heartfelt
Longing for light? Why grovel again and again
In darkness and pain when now and always
The Light is within you? Turn inwards then,
Turn around and face the Light, thy True Way.

1949

THE TREE

There the tree stands, a signature of God:
Mighty and terrible and wonderful the force
That fashioned it to life from the sod
And a love-borne seed nestled at the source
Of nurture and growth, sucking at mighty-breasted earth.
Love was its conception, the uniting of things diverse
To bring a form so beautiful into flowering birth,
The forces that make thee tree, the wide world traverse.

1950

GOD AND THE MOMENT

The living of life is an agony
Of time before and time to come.
Only in the moment lies the remedy,
In the Self engrossed in passion
For each moment, greedily drinking
At the fount of life, the passing
Of the present. In time stopped
Lies God; not in worries from the past
Nor revelations of the future.
This is our realization at the last,
At the bitter end of struggle.
"Live in the now; it is golden."
The Voice of God speaks thus;
See His finger through all events,
Each a direct dealing with the soul,
Each a lesson no forethought prevents,
Each an inkling of our goal.

1950

CREATION (II)

Analysis steals away the body of an art.
My lords, I must create, and wilt thou say me nay?
Those who have not spirit nor heart,
Who cold, unthinking, speakest what they say,
And only heed the world and not the highest voice;
Who say it of the outside and not of Inner Self.
My lords, I say the artist has no choice;
He must damn thee for scriveners,
For men who own a lack,
Mere grovelers upon the ground
Who can nor will not feel of Beauty's rack;
But who must instead devour her face
And smother all in words that turn
Against her grace.

Oh, let me be an artist
And turn my scorning eye
Upon the dissecting words of men
That disgrace the heaven high
    Of love's creation.

Oh, let me burn my life out
And turn a deafened ear
To those who would speak of me,
Be it harm or cheer,
    Of my creation.

I would live unknowing
Of the tearing up of life
And the wars of words upon my work.
Begone! thou dogs that lurk
    'Gainst my creation.

                        1952

THE FLOWER OF EROS

With a torn and bleeding heart
   And bowed head I pass by
On eternal course; as a star that wheels
   Through the naked, tortured sky.
Oh, Eros, pitiless God, that set
   The stars and I amid the glitter
Of fallen tears and the fret
   Of an anguished cry.

Oh, Eros, pitiless God! No end is there
   To Thy flaming dart which pierces
The center of my being and sends
   Me reeling along my course, like Circe's
Lover transformed into swine; blindly
   Caught and enmeshed in desire with faces
Set against the divine. Oh, Eros! See
   Thy ravaging traces!

And yet there lies hidden in Thy play
   A breath from the heaven of soul.
A breath which whispers through shadow
   And tears of a shining magical Whole.
If the pain of love is so great and it kindles
   The heart into flame so that life
And death are the same and mingle
   As joy and sorrow unroll:

If there is heard a call from the forces
    Which unwind the unraveling thread
Of light and darkness; the spiral of play,
    The pathway of life on which the feet tread:
If the call is so great that it shatter
    The tower of living so carefully built;
If love becomes all that matters
    And the sacrifice is blood:

And Thy face, Eros, once laughing and gay
    Behind the poisoned darts, changes and grows
Into a whispering roar, a presentiment
    Of that greater God, the One that goes
From tower to tower and razes them all
    With laughter divine and crazy and plays
A song of silence and speech and His call
    Like light through eternity flows:

And Death is nearest to Love and embraces
    The living heart; and the spirit is torn
By the struggle of forces and the fire
    Has left nothing but ashes. Within is born
Unshadowed Light, Godlike, virgin and pure,
    Rooted among the swine, but the Spirit
Enflamed to Nirvana. Then Thy flower,
    Oh, Eros! Life's Cross adorns!

1953

FORBIDDEN LOVE

Cruel love, thou appearest in a thousand faces;
The heart blossoms under thy approving glances;
The heart trembles and recoils from thee unaware
And calls upon the fates to undo thy traces.

Love, strike me not now or I despair:
Oh, I despair under thy smooth caresses,
Thy rapturous passion, thy intense kisses.
No, I cannot love, the impossible must remain afar.

Hush, be still my heart, do not leap at a sign
That is only another face among the crowd,
Another love, another passion, but oh, not mine.
Enclose me still my tight drawn shroud.

Is it not enough, those who have gone before?
Those whom I loved until the soul shivered in pain.
Can I not look now to thy power's wane;
Can I not cease, must I adore?

Cruel love, thou strikest me with thy torment.
I must prepare my face against betrayal;
Must still my heart against his arrival;
Be impersonal, cold, keep emotions pent.

Within a tight coiled purpose my serious age
Like unto a gray browed hermit, eremite,
Firm set against folly and gloried by an inner sight
And helped by His Light, as befits a sage.

1953

THE ARROW AND NUIT

The arrow is feathered and plumed:
    It awaits its flight
Preening and whispering and poised,
    Eager to fly.
Its point is barbed and stained,
    Deadly poisoned
Point of desire, quivering there
    And ready to aim.
Oh, Nuit, lay open your bosom,
    Graciously receive
Our desire, our high flung effort
    To your pearly abode.
Nuit, Lady of the stars
    And of the vacant night.
Catch up the arrow and wring out
    Its life blood.
The cup of Nuit is shimmering and ready:
    The cup of Her body
Open to catch blood dewdrops
    Dropping from life
And love's effort. See how the cup
    Swallows it up
And all is gone - yet there remain
    Ashes and dust and Silence.

1954

SILVER & GOLD

Cup of gold and thread of silver,
Peace of skies, half mist formed
And lazy. These are found in better eyes
    Than mine.

Cup of gold, a happy omen:
Thread of silver weaving through
My heart. Thin tendrils of silver become
    A sign.

And the cup of gold is a tender moment
A wistful look, a promise that leaps
In glances. Silver and gold together caught
    And entwined.

                           1954

WAITING

My eyes open in surprise and joy:
There it is that has been hidden;
There the rapture, there the gold
Of life. There are those golden feet
Whispering through the sands of time.
See how the forbidding wall has fallen,
The stark restriction unrealized now.
The wall has broken apart and the key
Has been relinquished to the unknown.
The citadel lies in ruins.
Only the suggestion of a whisper,
Only the strange and muted song
Of love: only a restrained echo
Breathing back and forth down corridors
Misty with lives unlived.
Only then the tenderness in hearts;
The silent rustle within a glance
And shimmering reflections in other eyes:
Only then and the door unlocks;
The walls are down and I wait.

1954

FORESIGHT

Though thou who foreseest for me Death,
Oh, my Soul, yet there is in your glances
A nimble spark of purpose
A hastening of Thy quick breath
As Thy rapture my body embraces.
Oh, Lord of Life, oh, glistening One;
Oh, Thou, who dealest alike joy and pain,
Oh, Thou Moon wedded to the Sun;
Oh, Thou whose quick finger traces
Paths of agony upon my breast;
Oh, Thou who wearest as Thy guise
Thy Presence in a thousand faces;
Who came to me on the wings of the morning
And left with the pulse of the first sunray
Thou who willed that I must walk these shadows
Through the false light of the blinding day;
Thou who caught me trembling into Thy arms;
Thou – Thou willed it, Oh, Soul of mine;
Thy mark of death is on my brow
And Thy cross of life my body adorns.

1954

WHAT JOY

What joy without thee?
The heart burns and trembles
At a quivering last look
And the wind blows up the sand.
What joy without the best
And fullness of life, a face
Faded into distance and all
Heartbeats wrung with pain.
What joy without the life
Of my soul, the full tremor
Of delight, the magic touch
Which soothed the frightened heart.
What joy on a joyful day
Surrounded by other voices
Happy and carefree. The full winds
Will never blow the same.

1955

MUSIC

Fleeting now is this essence of life
Forming in clouds in the empyrean.
Oh, Joy, that hovers near and hidden,
Sharp poignant thrust as a knife
Slicing trough a heart shaken
By sounds sweet beyond those solemn
And majestic, slow-moving clouds
That ride the twilight wind;
Forming ever a rose and a blue of heaven.

Fitting accompaniment to a moment
This symphony of cloud and sound.
Fitting expression of music that foments
Tender love in the glittering round
Of eternal Joy. Oh, Life, Oh, Love,
Oh, Beauty existing timeless and free
For the heart reaching along and among
The agonies of suffering. Now purified, sees
The eternity of joy that lies in a song.

1956

THE VALLEY OF TRAGEDY

We walk ever in the valley of tragedy.
The great Muse who rules over that place,
Brooding sadly, her eyes dimmed with tears,
Glittering raindrops of pellucid brightness,
Slowly formed and wrung from a heart in pain,
Walks in cloud-formed shadow and brushes by.

Glittering raindrops on a pallid cheek;
A figure shrouded in clouds of dark brightness,
Tragedy in the clouds that hang low;
Clouds that shoot forth gleams
From under the passing of the dark figure
Ever brooding over her valley.

And this is our valley of tragedy.
The dark mists rise to meet the clouds;
The forms approach and depart before ever
They are seen. Dark forms wrapped in mystery.
Ah, perhaps there goes a bright light,
A soul holding a candle of brightness.

But no, this is the Valley of Death,
And the soul departs before ever it is known.
Now the yearning one reaches out a hand
To break through the barrier of mist.
But there is nothing to touch,
Only a swirling and retreating cloud.

Hear how a hollow laugh rings out wildly
And a drop of moisture falls near.
Still there is silence in the waiting heart.
The silence grows and a question is whispered low,
But nothing answers and there forms
Another shining drop from that brooding mist.

1956

NEPTUNE

The longing of the heart is never quenched,
Waiting in the silence left by absence.
The night stars glitter and answer nothing,
Shedding pale gleams on an anguished cry.

The dark whirls and envelopes all the song
Sung by the soul in loneliness, and far –
Far the stars travel, pale listeners
To all that reaches out on the wings of a sigh.

Eternity blows through the heart and there
Reigns the kingdom of loneness reaching
Forever into the heights of night darkness
And the terror of going forever is nigh.

Pale strands of light that bid love,
Attenuated and thin, reach across distances
On wings of sound and warmth of human love
Shunts out the night and the vision of loneliness dies.

1956

THE END (I)

The end of an era will strike
In a room quiet with talk.
An exchange of confidence and laughter
Can lead suddenly to the end.

Glad the heart was when approaching
Blood coursing wildly in the veins,
Calm head belying the unquiet heart,
A heart that gave the game away.

When suddenly amid the talk and laughter
Like a snake waiting coiled to strike,
There shone for deadly minutes a hate
And the heart faltered and wavered.

A surprise sprang full blown and cold.
Could it be so? asked the heart:
And the cold hand of dread answered
It is so, it is true, it is the end.

1957

45

SOLILOQUY

A strange being walks the earth
Disguised in chains of flesh;
Lost to heavenly Self and bound
By laws of Karma. So walks
The hidden light. But joy
Of brilliant sunshine illuminates
The darkness of the day
And flames of fire flicker
Within the hidden heart.
A glory surrounds the earth
Kneeling dark and unheeding.
Black is the soil heaving
With hidden life. Clouds of heaven
Gather and darken day unto fitful night.
So run events for the Angel soul
As the dark earth are events,
As clouds that frighten the sky.
And the spirit shudders and cries,
"Woe! There is bitter loneliness
And darkness and hateful terror across
The face of the Earth.
Deep and heavy clouds and furies gather
To shake the heavens and rush
Wildly through affrighted air and beneath
They rumble through ancient earth.
With laments and cries man dies in chains

Of lust and flesh and appetites."

The spirit, shaking, cries thus and is afraid.
Miasma and fears darken the inner world;
Smearing events like veils across that Self.
Regrets return, ancient wrongs knell fury
And black death hovers o'er the torture.
The should is lost, vainly shaking its chains.
O should that forges thine own chains!

Above the clouds the luminous air carries
The smiles of the sun ever shining
Upon the teeming earth.
A wearied man, scarcely guessing, looks up
To catch the splendor of sun dimly seen
Through the drifting and changing mists.
"Oh, shining sun!"

Always the Angel is behind the should.
Always a flame burns within.
Events are clouds that come and go
And the Angel cannot be chained or lost.
"Angel, depart not because of the clouds!"
"Man, thou art that angel"
Is the eternal reply.

1957

TO JANE

Oh, I could weep for time gone by
When golden feet walked through my days,
And wisdom whispered words as a sigh
Lifted and enlightened my heart.

Your feet, my Jane, have trod earth and gone.
Your voice heard no more. And yet lingers
As a ghost, the perfume and the song
Of your presence lingering on in old papers.

Your legacy to me, your child, a pile
Of dusty manuscripts. And there is the task
Of compiling, sorting, reading, the while
You gently smile in the sleep of death.

Your gentle presence belied your will of steel;
Born yet to wander and become confused.
Still I may inherit your wisdom and feel
The wild wind of freedom caressing my heart.

"I failed," you sighed, and never forgave yourself that.
And I told you "not so," for work had been done.
Now there is the legacy and what
Remains of your purpose. Yes, I inherit.

1957

STRANGE HEART

Strange heart and its reflections
As in a limpid pool of crystal
Of the Angel in all His perfections.

Strange heart full of music soaring
As if all the sounds of heaven
Were through one frail vessel pouring.

Strange heart now wayward wandering;
Alas! thirsting for earthly joys,
Vehicle of music clouded and floundering.

Then strange music pouring from heart's wounds
As if God must speak through sorrow.
Still an Angel song when the last note sounds.

1959

CONVERSATION

Oh, Great One of the Night of Time
Night is but the absence of Thy Light.
"Say you so? Fool! for fine
And unfine, night and day are mine."

"Night is farther removed from Me
As a stone is farther removed from man.
But all begin and end in my Unity.
Turn thy face to thy Creator, oh man."

A most precious gift does He bring
And what were doubts and terrors of night
Become glittering dewdrops on a string
Of events foreordained from eternity.

1965

THE MYSTIC

Sometimes I am whipped into a frenzy
And the desire to know – to know – comes upon me.
I must be flaming, be learning, be reading, finding out.
Friends I must have and all the business flowing 'round about.
Life must whirl and inform and yield before me;
I must know and understand, must laugh and speak again.
In question must touch hand to hand;
Must love deeply and know pain.
Must know pain and joy as one delight of vivid life.
But then I recoil as a spring.
Bent from so much exertion and strife.

Of two minds is the recoiling and the leaping;
Of two minds the venturing forth to know and the return.
Even as a pendulum is the joyous will outgoing
And its return again to a quiet, still in knowing.
And here, quiet, deep, alone, half asleep, it lies
Seeking to understand what lies beneath life's phenomena.
So I, touching stained hand upon the fecund earth;
Wild deeds and thoughts forgotten, of joy and flame a dearth;
All actions suspended from me between heaven and earth,
Wait, and waiting I work at weeding, and wait to know.
Wait for the knowing to strike me, as working slow
I listen to the quiet run of thoughts buried deep but meaningful
Of something stirring in unknown depth of being: as yet dull,
As yet unperceived, but some mystery still to slant

From out of impervious depths. Then in a moment so scant
There is scarcely room to breathe or to sigh,
A striking knowledge comes upon me and all the sky
Rends open with the voice of knowing and with great light;
Which I waited for so long and delved so deep to hear,
Which I yearned for so blindly and strove for, despite
Hard aguish of word and pain, more striving than I could bear.
Released, the pain and joy equilibrated thus
In moment of knowing from out of mind darkness
I am free again; free to begin again
My wild search for knowledge, child of my brain.
Oh, Lord, let me understand Thy unseen Universe.

1965

END OF DAY

Golden light at the end of day
Caught in the limbs of the alder.
Golden heart a willingness to display
Tangled with others in great order.

Fierce are the birds in their nesting
Songs of warning in Springtime.
Fierce is my heart in the darkening
Shutting of day into purple nighttime.

Young sound the birds in their song of dusk
As gold fades to dull and evening creeps on.
Tired is my heart and full of distrust,
For age and the night have left me alone.

1969

FLOWERS

Sweet lavender of the lilac
And heavy maroon of prunus, oh see
White narcissus bowing its head
Over its own water reflection.

Heavy sits the rain on flower and leaf
Blasting and browning tender azalea
But gently loving the primrose
Who lifts her head in greeting.

In passion I am become as the lilac
Loving dark leaf of prunus.
Delicate and pale lilac florets
Poised against dark hue of blood.

And I am narcissus bending
Not for my face but for thine.
Bend over me then, and we two
Shall see ourselves and Pan in the water.

As the azalea I become blasted
And shattered by the desire of Pan
Oh help me to be as the primrose
To lift my head and drink His Force.

1969

54

RAINDROPS

The rain kisses pink illumined petals
Of tulips and nestles close within a flower's heart.
Alabaster tulips and rosy ones, but mortal
As am I. In love I am become part
Of them, even as a cupped tulip palace.

Ah, my Lord, I cup these whitened hands
And gather within them dew of heaven.
Clear, like receptive water I stand
Holding this offering for your: undine driven
By love to form for thee this silent chalice.

Then the crystalline beauty of raindrops
Falls into cupped magnolia leaf.
There a little bird preens and flops
In tiny pool, and like a thief
Pushes away the accretion of water.

So come then and skirmish in this pool
As does the bird; and should you cease,
Look deep within the drops and see the crystal
Of heavenly light gathered here to please
My God of Love. Raindrops for a satyr.

1969

55

MYSTICAL MARRIAGE

A delicate flower lies here in this grass
Torn from root-stem, petals askew,
Plucked trembling and fearful, and oh, alas!
Thrown down and forgotten and wet with dew.

The night sky shudders and trespasses here
And soft finger caresses silken edged surface.
In wonder and delight I press my face near
To see night and flower in mysterious symbiosis.

The night and the flower become one in me;
Mystical marriage of delicate lightening.
We all are one in the starry eternity,
And I, like the flower, am crumpled and waiting.

The grass prickles up against my flesh,
Pinwheels whirling before my eyes,
Each nerve upended under this stress
Of spiraling light raining down from the skies.

My flesh creeps with cold faery light:
The dew on the ground runs through my being
And I am ecstatic here in this night,
Opening as a flower to the God ever seeing.

My fingers clutch earth, then raised overhead.
As I gaze into deep eyes scattering mine.
I spread and curl fingers around your head
And pull down stardust in moment sublime.

1969

INVOCATION

Adonai, Lord, come to me on the wings of Love.
Brilliant should-self, interior light, white dove,
I adore Thy breath, soul of night and stars.
Thou are my star-self, thou canst undo the bars.

Far, far, deep within the faint glimmer of your light
Approaches to my conscious mind and pure delight
Breaks over my being; gone is the barrier of thought;
Mind annihilated, see what you have wrought.

I am a pure virgin in your Light; how I have longed
For Thy presence, and now events that have thronged
Through this life are melted in your fiery crucible.
Of strong desire; Thou who art the Holy One, adorable.

Adonai, I am a grail that Thy spark I might receive,
White clothed, worshipful, Thy presence I retrieve
Yet again from Thy lurking place in my soul.
Light divine, come to me and again make me whole.

As a red rose I await your passionate kiss;
Come and wrap me away in your unending bliss.
By Thy presence do Thou unfurl my petals wide,
Golden One of Song, come now to my side.

As a lyre I await Thy plucking, honeyed voice
Stirring the tuned strings of my desire. Ah, I rejoice
As Thy soft feet approach nigh, your Angel wing
Brushes my brow, Enfold me while I sing.

Adonai, Spirit of delight, of bliss transcending.
Adonai, my love for Thee has been unending.
Thy faintest voice has perfumed my soul;
Speech and Silence has been yours as aeons unroll.

Break open this shell; transcend the bonds of mind;
Ravish my being, pull away the material blind.
Show Thy Star-nature, whilst my foundations are shaken.
Adonai answers this my call. He loves and I am taken.

1969

THE ROSE OF LOVE

The rose gleams in the wildwood,
Silvery dewdrops on petals lie,
Red and green diamond-glitters brood
In the heart of the flower
    And so do I.

The fern, soft green and glistening,
Tendrils unfolding to wide sky,
Scatters drops of dew, deepening
The color of scattered leaves;
    And there am I.

Fresh breezes assault my nostrils
Wafting pine smell as they pass by;
And so I wait, a poetic wastrel;
Waiting until my soul stirs;
    Ah, I could die.

Oh, Adonai, Steal close to me
On the life of the breeze, draw nigh
To my parched heart and see
How I wait as the rose does!
    I wait, even I.

I am the flower, petals unfurled,
My red heart blown open, a sign
Of love on my lips, dewdrop pearled
With impressions of senses. Thou'rt hidden
       And where am I?

Thy finger traces its fire upon my breast.
I whirl and dance; I reach to the sky.
So suddenly has Thy caress blessed
My heart now aflame with love.
       A flaming fire am I.

I am the red scented rose and Thou
Art my essence; I am no longer I.
We are wed, we are blessed, allow
My this moment of bliss. Thou art.
       I am no longer I.

Oh essence, Oh, dewdrop, oh pearl;
The Dweller in the abode that is I.
Oh, light at the heart of creation's curl,
Curving inward in delight. I am Thou
       And Thou art I.

1970

THE SOLDIER AND THE QUEEN

Courageous soldier who thus faces
The dread Queen, the terrible twin,
Now mild, now mystery in trances
Between her eyes, whose ennui begins
And vanishes, whose passion flares and dies.
Happiness smothered in a smile.
Ah, soldier, you are patient with her signs;
Come, sit beside me awhile.

A Queen who does not know her own mind.
Perforce must ask directions of thee.
'Tis whispered that love is blind;
When you are here, how could that be?
Oh, laugh, if love the Queen you must;
Then delicate tenderness and flame
Spring within you of joyous lust.
Invoke the Moon, I shall become tame.

The Star of Venus diademed on my brow,
Yet hidden behind petulant veils
Of thoughts, eyes dark and hollow;
I reel between dark and light, the pale
Of impulsive mine. Courageous thou art
To view this swaying Queen of Love
In Patience, to take no active part
For or against her mind's treasure trove.

Tomorrow all is swept away
Of the mind's glittering images.
There is no truth in this brilliant play
Of opposites; as torn and bleeding pages
In the Book of Life, all prostrate
Before One truth; Center of my Being.
Courage! unmask me before its too late;
For I am Love before thee fleeing.

1970

A PAEAN

I await the awaking! the summons on high
From the Lord Adonai, from the Lord Adonai!
— Liber LXV, Cap. I, v.1

O Beloved and my only Master
O Splendid One with the wings of a Dove
Empearled and glittering;
I await, my heart beats faster
At the wing sounds swirling above,
Oh dewy One, I am dancing.

On the wings of song you approach:
Daffodils bend their heads
Swaying before Thy fresh breath,
Thou essence of perfume, touch
My brow, my worldly cares are shed
Far into the abyss, a part of death.

For aeons have we loved, draw nigh
And pledge our love once again
In honeyed kiss. I await Thy bliss.
Thou who art rapture, who art I
In my unknown essence, 'tis in vain
If ever I turn from Thee, my soul's bliss.

Great star nestled in Nu's bosom
United we are one, we are none
In Her starry light, enchanted
By Her sorcery, hearts blossom
Amongst her stars: not alone
Are we, but streams of light slanted

From star to star. Each angel sends
Light essences of ineffable love:
Each love an ecstasy of Nuit.
The star ray dazzling my eyes bends
Before Thy gaze, oh tender dove,
Lady of the Stars, Oh, Nuit.

1970

DAY OF MIRTH

Crystal are the sounds in the air
As the soft tender eve approaches nigh.
Ah, day that was so healing and fair
As the warm sun kissed and stole by.

A birdsong of beauteous delight
Enchants and entrances my heart.
Ah, bird, thou art so fairy bright
Caroling as you perch and then dart.

I too am a small bird for my love,
Caroling sweet songs for his ear,
Or perhaps I am a white dove
Fluttering wildly as he comes near.

Transformed, I am a Queen
Bearing gifts from the earth.
Oh, love, where have you been
To have lost this day of mirth?

1970

SONGBIRD

A broken songbird upon a bough
Sits sad and disconsolate, wings clipped,
Song muse gone, life not to allow
The joy of former years. All love slipped

Into oblivion, and toil the favor of soul-night.
When lo! Unto the senses straining
For break of dawn, breaks the light,
Great Sun on rim of the world, streaming

Fingers of life into soul of silent bird.
And now bursts forth a praising paean
Of love-song, like unto none ever heard
Save in the God-soul of the aeon.

1970

STAR PLAY

Oh, beloved One and my only Master,
Oh, splendid One with the wings of a Dove;
Impassioned, empearled and glittering
I await Thee.
My heart beats faster At the wing sounds swirling above.
I faint, oh, dewy One, Thou art entrancing.

On the wings of song I hear you approach
As bright daffodils bend their heads
Swaying before Thy fresh breath,
Thou Essence of perfume. Oh, touch
My brow. My worldly cares are shed
Far into the abyss, a part of death.

For aeons upon aeons we have loved; draw nigh
And pledge our beatific love once again.
As I await Thy touch in honeyed kiss,
Thou who art silent rapture, who art I
In my unknown Essence. It is in vain
If ever I turn from Thee, my soul's bliss.

Great One, a point nestled in vast night's bosom;
We are One, and in ourselves also None;
By the ancient starry light enchanted.
Voluptuous in Her sorcery, hearts blossom

Amongst Her stars. See then, not alone
Are we; our loves are streams of light slanted

From star to star. As the Holy Angel sends
Light essences of ineffable love,
As each love is an ecstasy of Nuit,
So the secret ray of my eyes bends
Before Her implacable gaze, oh tender dove,
Our Lady of the Stars, mysterious Nuit.

1970

TRANSCENDING

What splinters the sky into a thousand tiny darks;
What perfume of roses and lavender etches itself apart;
What sweet earth is this upon which I walk;
And what gentle stream amidst the stones in whispering talk?

Sweet is the sky in blue and purple enclosing me here,
Long rays reach out from the stars fairy clear,
The full bright moon whispers her secret ecstasy
Against the velvet night and I burn with empathy.

Sweet is the gift of life amidst the gardens and the roses
Ecstatic is the song wafting along the breeze that blows.
Ah, Lord, 'tis a Paradise on the dark benign earth,
Ours is the transmutation of sense, ours the love, ours the mirth.

Oh, birth of Joy, springing out of the gates of hell;
The underworld of dark emotions melts under Thy spell.
Gone are the frustrations and the sad world of fear.
Oh, ravish me away in ecstasy; I feel Thy presence near.

Blue and silver gilt sparkle down the skies in whirling motion,
Ancient Love since before the world began or rolled the ocean,
Fire and brooding water since the æons primeval,
Ah, come to me, sing to me, Thy song of beauty eternal.

In Light transcending and transforming this world I celebrate
In paeans of praise, in arcs of forms, on Thy wine inebriate.
Oh, Splendor of Glory, Thou has caught me up in Thy Light,
I – a tiny spark in thy vast abode, swoon in delight.

1971

THE END (II)

The year is tumbling down into November:
Brave leaves fall sadly upon the earth.
Must my heart so sorrowfully remember
The blasting of sweet hopes after love's birth?

The dried and puckered leaves scatter widely:
Their yellow fades to brown, a dull foretaste
Of days of regret, of slow death entering mildly
And quickening to finish the year in unctuous haste.

I relied on you and loved you, clinging as a leaf
To the strength of your bough proudly held.
Our hearts were Springtime together as a sheaf
Of flowers sweet scented and wild in one delightful meld.

But the year passed on and age struck close.
Winter sent a warning note as you froze my heart.
Non-caring in your ways and non-tender as you chose.
I, the tender leaf, saw the end and so fell apart.

1974

THE ALCOHOLIC

I am in full flight, torn
In my depths, heart shorn
Of tenderness, mind and fangs bared
To return ill for ill shared.

Daily I watch the degeneration
Alcohol brings, a fool's summation
Of life, a past still clutching
At mind and soul, a spirit retching.

The devious arguments in favor
Of a practice so degrading, the savor
Of each chilled bottle is more than honour,
More than life, more than love's fervor.

Poor slave to alcohol, who counts as nothing
The joys of health, the full flowering
Of a mature and healthy mind,
As he kills each brain cell in excess blind.

Poor slave, who gladly passes by
A full flowering of love, nightly
Drinks and prevents competence in bed.
Ah, slave, is your heart dead?

And I, who suffer most, must bear
Reproaches for love's failure there.
Dear one, how can I continue thus?
Must I be victim to your drink lust?

Uncomprehending victim of drink
How is it that soul could sink
So low as to lose all powers of will?
Does not the conscience speak still?

How, if things on this earthly plane
Be not controlled, can you deign
To rise so high in your ambition
As to seek the utmost soul's fruition?

How is it that you can honor forsake
In favor of a bottle, and hope to take
The highest rewards of leadership
When good example comes not from lip

Not from what is said, but from what is done.
Leaders who no example show stand alone.
Headlong fall thus built into Nature's law.
The sage only is fit to lead, not the man of straw.

And I, despairing, mind and heart torn;
Alone in depths of misery, quite forlorn
And unloved, must still my tongue

Lest I make wrong more wrong.
Inwardly I cry, is this love?
Does not love endure all, a trove
Of suffering and forbearance, a haven
Kind and gentle, a forgiving heaven?

Ah, yes, love forgives and love strikes.
Both emotions in one, they are alike;
Hate and love are twain endurance;
Show fight blended with true romance.

And so suppressing gentler desires,
Tenderness, pity must now suspire
On my altar of flame, love's strength
Through tribulation of ordeal of great length.

Must I suffer thus? I raise my head.
No! my spirit and will are not dead.
So, risking all on one deadly throw
Of dice, I gird myself for the blow.

My love, I thus present my case.
I can so kill my heart for a space;
Be alone, should you so decree.
I vow, take the drink or take me.

But you may not have both.
I too can hit at the bonds of our troth
As do you in your blind absorption
In little self, your aversion to love's fruition.

Thus as courageous Amazon I stand still
Girded with the sword of Will.
Heart burning on it and emblazoned below,
"A leader is not unless example show."

A leader and man you are not to me;
My soul mate must stronger be.
No slave to sense, no alcoholic souse
Can win me as his spouse.

I hope you may win to the Golden Bough.
The King's Daughter awaits your vow.
Be a warrior still, flaming sword in hand;
Arise above the slave state and stand

Master of self, wand of Will cleansed
And dedicated anew, lower and higher blends
In one-pointed Will, when awaiting thee
With silver cup, a goddess will be.

1975

SPRING

Will you accept Spring into your heart?
The winter's night has gone away.
But I sit here alone and apart
My love has not chosen to stay.

Will you accept Spring into your blood?
Dry and withered and old I cry,
"Is Spring then to do me good
When all life burgeons only to die?"

Can you let Spring flow through your hair?
Standing free, but heart within its wall.
Can Spring's light birdsong reach your ear?
If love is gone, how can I hear at all?

1975

ETERNITY'S LAIR

Soft footfall echoes along the edges of space;
Eternal verity of love plagues the knower
As willful feet slowly stride apace
And athwart the ancient Ways of the viewer.

Oh, gentle leaves supported on stems
And trunks of trees deeply rooted in earth,
Leaves dappled with shade and shining rims
Glistening in sun. All beauty speaks forth.

Soft beauty of life suffuses the mind and soul
As I pace slowly through gentle air.
Like unto a raindrop, one part of the whole
Waits to merge in Water, soul laid bare.

The soul awaits, open to all, open to love
And dreaming to catch eternity in a kiss:
While stretching greenly far above
The limbs of trees intertwine in bliss.

Nature awaits with open arms and tender smile
With direful thunder and lightning and heavy clouds;
With rain lashing and bending leaves while
The joyful heart welcomes all and sings aloud.

The birdsong and the delicate frog are there
Waiting as expressions of a soul bemused
By such perfections of form and who would dare
Strain forth all senses into eternity's lair.

1976

TO A MAGNOLIA

I see a crumpled petal of purity
Of white magnolia shining in the sun.
A sunbeam kisses away its serenity
And a dappled shade its whiteness overcomes
Whilst gently swaying among its leaves alone.

Sweet and gentle breezes fondle its silk,
Cup creamy white and heavily scented,
Whiter even than the white of milk.
Now blown by the breeze and slanted
The heavy leaves encompass it around.

Like thee, magnolia, I am afloat, afloat,
Hungering ever for the kiss of day
And folded tight against the coming night.
Oh, blissful white, pearly, secure, oh stay!
Stay magnolia, my heart surround.

Thy image sears itself against my brain
As I gaze into thy hungering depths;
Thy form cupped to receive a gentle rain.
Visiting insects assert their troths
With thy lambent light newly found.

Oh, pure magnolia, surely the unseen hand
That set thee there on thy tree
Is also the hand that reflected and fanned
Thy blaze of purity in my soul. May I be
Forever cupped, to Eternity betrothed and bound.

1976

DREAM PHENOMENA

Time to let the dawn creep upon my soul;
Time to let the sun fling its rays athwart my eyes;
Time, oh, time again to let the daytime roll
O'er mind blissed with sleep, o'er sleepy sighs.

The march of day begins against my will;
The sun sharply climbing up the sky,
The dawn breeze blows and seeks to fill
With filmy evanescence my thoughts as I lie.

From emptied mind the dreams flee out-shrieking
Whilst vain regrets to know their presence gone
Slimes o'er the soul that would fain again be sleeping
Until fair dreams have pushed aside the dawn,

Mystic thoughts arise to meet the oncoming light of day.
The light shatters and steals down the tracks of mind.
Birdsong rips apart the veils; oh, who can say
The ultimate reality of either of these kind?

Mocking bird that mocks my hold on sleep;
Delirious notes beat against half-closed ears
And I relinquish slowly illusions I desired to keep
From among the flotsam of the dream world, the soul's tears.

Gentle on my mind the nymphs play in and out
Along the shafts of breath that help to shape the dreams
And I lie quiescent as the dreadful doubt
Beseeches my soul to question what it seems.

Is life a dream? or are dreams become reality?
What is real? Oh, Gods, you have your way
When dreams lead us to your thrones with such dread fatality
And we bow to your power until the outspoken light of day.

Neglect not the dawn meditation, oh sleepy brain.
Surely some transcendence will push away the day
Until all splinters into Light, the mind drained
Of ancient phenomena and the heart eager for the play.

1977

THE TOMB OF THE WEST

Night with its soft radiance of dreams
    Steals o'er the sky pushed by the wind,
Harbinger of relief to the tired eye
    And daily toil and labour grim of mind.

Night with its soft mantle of stars
    Creeps upon my mind and heart in sly
Silken movements; moving against the bar
    Of consciousness: To sleep is to die.

The hallowed dusk that heralds velvet night
    Beats upon my senses and creates motion
Unto rest and repose as the swift flight
    Of birds ceases over restless ocean.

When night announces her return from the end of day,
    Oh, evening star, dost thou present a promise
Of heavenly glories that swallow up my Way
    In the vast expanse of heaven's bliss?

When I too shall shut down my day on earth
    And step into the other side of life, pure love
Of night and stars expanding soul's girth
    In death: with only memories as my treasure trove.

1978

THE PRESENCE

Ah, my Lord, I see Thee in the rainbow in the spray;
I see Thee in the gentle sun of reclining day;
I know Thee in the breezes which ride through the trees
And in the muted hum of intoxicated bees.

I see Thee in the glistening green of leaves rejoicing
In moisture of water striking gently and moistening
Their surface of calm. I see Thee, O Lord in the bluejay there
And hear in his raucous call yawked forth on air.

I know Thee in the space and skies that yawn above;
I hear Thee in the calm, cool, calling of the dove.
Thy Presence stalks through my life and sleep;
 I know Thee, Lord, through Thy call from out my deep.

I know Thee, O Lord, in the inner Light sprung forth,
An eidolon of the Sun which each must bring to birth.
I see Thy Hand in my multitudinous eventful ways;
I see Thy purpose glimmering throughout all my days.

As jewels in the sun and in the night of space
I found Thee, Lord, as Thou dost run apace
This starry grained matter, this essence
Of life and light and love worshiping Thy lovely Presence.

O, Lord, be my helper to know Thee in all Thy Ways,
In every grain of matter, in every thought that plays
Through my mind. Oh, bring the intoxicating vision,
The lessons that tear and bind until I make the decision

To know no other through all events upon this earth;
To know that Thou art behind this joyful birth
Of spirit sprung from the interplay of light and dark,
That Thou dost sing within me as some most heavenly lark.

1978

STORM (I)

The wind whirled upon my open page:
The tempest swirled through its last stage
Across my book. Darkness descended upon my abode
As I entered therein against night's mode.

My book is the book of my heart, oh love,
And you as one page of its truth drove
As a storm against its whiteness; a stain
On the present sanctity of heart's disdain.

Storm gathered over the sky in the blackening night;
Rain beat its tattoo on my heart like a blight
Snuffing out its eagerness. Ah, what a blame
Crouches curled and crawling through a world of shame.

Dread and terror leap o'er a precipice of fears.
Can you not see how your opinion openly sears
Against old wounds and a terrible heart's rending
Swirls out in emotional storm unending.

Breaks the lightening and the heart is cleansed of tears:
Clouds are chased onward until a rift appears
And a Star shines through; a pale soft light
Heralding the wonder of storm-riven night.

I hear the message clearly in contrast of star and storm.
Life is not as it appears to be in form
Of emotions tortured and torn. Life is calm and clear
As a Star's path through heavens far and near.

1979

WHIRLINGS

The Universe opens up in whorls upon whorls
Of energy, the interfacing of the Gods,
Their under-over-bending, unknown sworls
And issues of human life wherever they've trod.

I see it all now as an issue fantastic
Of never-ending dance through all eternity
Of lover and loved one in perfume of mastic
Conjoined and inseparable through an amenity

Of wedded bliss: Angel and human self
Divinely intertwined in ageless wisdom
Beyond phenomena, life, beyond belief,
Beyond emanations of the Tree and the Kingdom.

Oh, speak to me now from Unconscious mind
Of our age-long love and Beauty divine
In unfathomed space and of our blind
And yearning affinity, justice so sublime

That it is hidden in event of soul's
Intervention in space with forces
So unknown and unrecognized as to whole
Meanings and uses and love's endurable traces.

A Holy Guardian Angel leads us thus
To consider His presence in all of light
And darkness, a never-ending plus
To all of life's minuses and sere defenseless plight.

Thus in inebriation and ecstasy we sense
His presence leading us on to eternity
Of events full of His forbidding essence;
In events of whatever kind we know His mastery.

He leads us onward to final consummation
Of the Mystical Marriage of Star-point Hadit
Ongoing to final and never-ending annihilation
Of little self in vast expanses of Nuit.

I am gone, whirled away in vast sea
Of creation, utterly blind to frightful day
And alone as the blasted, lonely Tree
That has spanned the abyss in frightful disarray.

I am shattered through all that I have known:
Now born anew for a vaster and wider throne
Ordained by Him. Oh, bliss of soul blown
By love insatiable, Oh Nuit, Hadit unknown

To mortal soul except in madness and cohesion
Of subject and object until all floats in empyrean
Of ancient and never-ending laws of attraction
Of self and not-self into final dissolution.

1980

ADORATION OF NUIT

I adore Thee, Nuit, adore the agonies and trials
I adore the deadly deep desperation,
The uneven sleepless nights, vials
Of Thy eternal loneliness in manifestation.

I adore Thee through all that happens.
I am a quintessence of soul set on fire,
A flaming up of inner aspirations,
Forming a true eidolon of a soul that aspires.

I adore Thee Nuit, I adore Thy sweet traces
Of ineffable love, hidden in unlimited space
And hidden in life's sorrowful faces.
I adore Thee through life's race.

O, golden and silver of life's mystic dawn!
We move as a faint spark of light in vast illumination;
Thus sparking and living know how we spawn
Phenomena and all its illusion.

I adore Thee, Nuit, oh vast expanding One
Of illimitable Space. I in Thy bosom a minute
Vestige of forgotten and unknown atom
Spell yet an end to notions of the finite.

Oh, vast blue Space, O signature of matter,
Oh unfulfilled in eternal grace!
Who yearn for dancing point of light, unshattered
By its law of gravity and place.

Still I adore Thee, adore Thee, adore Thee,
Everlasting management possibilities.
Adore Thy oneness and interpenetration of me
Adore Thy ineffable harmonies.

Oh, plentiful agency of limitless beauty
I adore Thee far into blue-dimpled night
I bend towards Thee in evanescent duty
As a spark to manifest life, love, liberty and light.

I adore Thee as my true soul steals forth;
I adore Thee in art and inspiration;
I adore Thee in all loves and silent mirth;
I adore Thee in quiet transformation.

I am a virgin earth unto Thy sublime expression,
A virgin Queen, Malkah unrecognized.
I adore Thy traces through me in secret recognition
Of Illumination at last by Thee franchised.

Oh, Nuit, Goddess of all and none
And one again, and whatever may be
On heaven and earth and all between.
Love Thee because I am Thy whole-made Tree.

In Thy dispensation I am seeing through
Thy veils of dance as disguised infinity
As mysterious as eagle that flew
Into thine Empyrean, dissolving his trinity.

A soul laid bare aspires yet again to Thy bosom
Amid all of illusions laid aside and abandoned
Until the least of these lead to love's fruition
Beyond all experience that may be fathomed.

Oh, Nuit, I in Thy embrace lie sere
And turned into Nothing, only a cenotaph
Marking my existence. Too glorious to bear
Is Nuit who annihilates thus even my path.

This path exists no more because swallowed
In essential space. I am the butterfly
Destroyed by Light, wings that were malleable
To circumstance are gone in ecstasy of death's blight.

I adore Thee, Nuit, Thou glorious One unfulfilled
Through every interstice of space.
Today and always this life is spilled
In ecstasy of Thine unwearying embrace.

1980

NUIT'S LOVE

Ah, dare if you will, in the body of Nuit
And give all and take all in one moment
Of time and event and make all-in feat
Of Magick. Ever thus do we foment

Events in space, in never-ending dance
Of momentous phenomena. Did you know then
That in a short and electric glance
Of Her who is all power, is penned

The events of eternity? Forever willed
And known aforetime by you and loved apace;
Foreordained and fashioned and filled
With love for Nuit in her fathomless space?

Let us all then in true Thelemic guise
Accept and welcome this Lady of Infinity,
Of space immeasurable, her distance a disguise;
And immolate our souls on Her whole Tree.

Oh, illimitable space, we are guided by thread-like
Intimations of our immortality against time
And event. Secure ever in the god-like
Knowledge of light, life, love and liberty sublime.

In the course of the soul everlasting, afar
Glimmers ecstasy on the cross of life;
No matter the sorrow, no matter the bar
To final dissolution and end of strife.

Ah, Nuit, of all the lives I lived alone;
Be in all these thine adoration and bliss
Of life supernal. Thy full love blown
Into far empyrean, into eternal kiss.

My ability to love is challenged and I throw
The whole of myself into the abyss of dark.
The motion unites the inner unknown
Gods of light-dark twins, their love's spark

Lighting my existence and enflaming
Soul in love divine, ancient and foreordained;
Hidden and deep within unconscious striving
For completion, and even though life maimed

This inner innocence, I travel triumphant,
Secure and knowing of the glorious light, rare,
Singular, alone, forever knowingly ancient
In Nuit's love all that may be or is or was, eternal Star.

1981

DEATH

Voices slanting out of the past
In whisper of rustling paper moldy
And crumbling and the beloved voiced
Of those I loved echo still.
    Within my heart.

All my emotions are wrung and tears hang
Behind dry eyelids. Oh, those of you
I love and shall not hear again!
My friends whom I love and love still
    Even though apart.

My friends, your echo through the letters
That lie within this box amid faint odor
Of aged paper still rings out strongly
Knelling departure and death
    And tears my heart.

Oh, my loved ones, is this now my pain
That I must so control and contain
My depth of feeling while you lived
That scarce emotion wrinkled my brow
    And so stilled my heart?

That now you are gone in death
I needs must regret that I did not
More strongly clasp you in my arms,
More warmth in handshake I did now express,
    Nor laid bare my heart.

How I love you still and reminder strikes
When these papers I cull and rustle:
And as they have power to evoke you
I am reminded of your voices and your ways
    And I cry, "Why apart?"

Cruel death, that brings with it a train
Of regrets and tears and voices stilled
Out of reality, even though they echo now
Within me. Cruel death to leave me with pain
    That clutches my heart.

When I too am gone, I shall join you
In that far land beyond mortal being.
But until then my young life must run its course
Even though years of parting still continue
    And tears me apart.

1982

THE LIGHT OF LIFE

I love Thee in all the star wrought graces of the skies;
    In the Isis of beauty that about me lies
Waiting for Thy touch of love to awaken in splendid flame
    The ever-coursing thunder of Thy name.

Oh, splendid One, Lord of mystery unspeakable
    Coursing through my veins in agony unbearable,
Oh, Light of Life in splendorous rapture of delight
    Fill my veins with life in mystical might.

As a slender mote in the strong sunbeam dances
    So dance I as a creation of Thy fancies.
These words of mine are but chaff upon the wind
    Compared to the intensity of Thy glance and mind.

Eternal Lord, bind my everlasting course with Thee
    From aeon to aeon for all eternity;
Closer to Thy heart that I be fit symbol
    Of encompassing love; hold me lest I tremble.

These words are poor that fall before Thy face,
    Lend me still of Thy intoxicating grace
That I may pour my heart out in Thy praise
    And joined with my Lord, remain a Star ablaze.

1982

THE PRESENCE OF SPRING

Far distant mountains lie like a caress
    on the misty horizon,
Pale, dusky blue, they widen the sense
    of space from this eyrie.
Rapture lies in my heart on the side of this hill
    while breezes blown
From Spring's fleeting presence
    wander through my heart fitfully.

Pale stretches of distant land end
    in the near garden of my choice:
Nature speaks to me in majesty
    of blossom and singing bird.
In all this beauty I revel, and am caught up
    into the echoes of Thy voice.
Oh, Nature! God! Holy Angel!
    who can say with impunity what is heard?

Flowers of yellow, gold and orange
    bespeak the splendors of the Spring:
They echo the golden meaning of the sun
    which sheds its loving light
On all that burgeons into growth,
    on birds nesting or on the wing,
On me as working here, I labour carefully
    to echo beauty with all my might.

Careful plans and work of gardener,
>dirt soiled but splendrous of intention
To praise my Lord through care of gardens
>and care of mine own soul;
To spend days of worship with the beautiful
>in Love's pure invention;
To praise the unknown Lord of Unity and unending Space,
>together a Whole.

Could I but arrange that mankind,
>blinded by greed and ambition,
Wholly lost-in strivings toward ambiguous goals
>and blindly astray
From the One True Light hidden
>in outpourings of Nature's bounteous mission
To aid all to the Source, the One, the center of Life,
>the Light of day.

Ah, could this be true, that one small soul,
>having found the Creator,
Could inspire the sad, the poor,
>the dispossessed, those wandering on earth;
Victims of their own crimes against the Spirit
>and lost now, perhaps forever,
To the wondrous voice of God echoing ecstasy
>of renewal and love's birth.

Ah! Souls! Friends! arise with me
    in praise of this marvelous majesty
Of perfumed distance, of warmth and light,
    of growth springing from dark soil.
Arise and praise this bounty which lends such hope
    and love eternally
For the taking. Arise! Find growth,
    love and ecstasy in your own soul!

1985

DEATH THE SAVIOUR

The flower fades, another takes its place.
Oh, death, fleeing forever from before my face.
What mysteries lie encompassed in thy sweep;
What angelic voice emerges from thy hooded deep?

What mysteries lie underneath the form of life?
What unravellings underneath the forms of strife?
What transformations must we reluctantly undergo?
To what mysterious powers must we unremittingly bow?

Oh, death, the mysterious saviour of the race;
The laws of life must encompass thy powers and embrace
The rule of change and transformation, of transcendence
Over all that went before, in thy spiraling dance.

Death that prances in skeleton shape among the dead;
 Forbid forever that we should exclaim and be afraid
For we die daily among the flowers and the roses.
We die daily upon the cross, horizontal and vertical crosses.

Life phenomena blooms upon the cross and dies again
Only to be resurrected in a changed and willed fashion
By those of us dancing on the dead body of chaos
True Will encompassing change and death, forever thus.

All must go, the body and the imperfections of the soul:
All must disappear before the god that devours
Our hopes and wishes, our lower selves, our manifestations
Into life, our karma,our silly holiday confrontations.

All must go before the illuminating dance of death:
All must disappear, even our love and faith
In the illimitable sources of our unrealized being
Before the breath of change and with blindfolded seeing.

We float onwards, unchallenged, unorganized and bereft
Of all that went before, now all that we have left
Is the one essential light, the sun of self unencumbered,
The essence of memory and experience is all our lumber.

For we come and go from life to life to know and experience
Only those events foreordained by ourselves in the life of sense
Foreordained by life eternal in the bosom of heaven
As we play out our wills, all errors by heaven shriven.

Life unto life and death unto death we dance forever
On the prone corpse of matter, dying not, changing ever
Under the law of love, the union of things diverse;
Thus we follow and accede to the laws of the Universe.

1987

SUN OF BEING

Let us open our hearts and minds to the Highest
And throw off the veil of negative existence.
Come, let us tread among the stars of the blessed
Let us control the evidence of happenstance.

Let us see the world as pure phenomena of Will
Formed by ourselves in our going.
Let us see Adonai's hand in everything, but still
A making by ourselves, our seeds sowing.

Upon the bosom of earth our deeds are awaiting
The flowering of earth's bounty in roots and seeds
In leaves, flowers and fruits in true trysting with experience,
A wholesome result of our deeds.

Whatever we do, there is no escape from growth,
There is no escape from nature's way.
The Law is that the soul must come forth
From delusion and terror to seek the light of day

The sun is our nurturance, our aim, our goal
Center of being, each one's life essence;
The sun is nature's law, of bounties untold;
The sun is in our hearts, a shield and defense.

The sun is our nature's pure being, a sensation
Reflected and absorbed in earth nature's breast.
We are that sun of being, that absorption
In the all, we are each a star in this feast.

Between sun and earth, own this grounding, this territory seen
As growth, our exploration of ourselves as a Hadit
The point of light nestled in the bosom of phenomena
An outcome of our wedding with and love for Nuit.

1991

STORM (II)

All of the darkened sky is riven
By lightning flash eerily driven
   By clouds heavy with water woe.

Ah me, but the clouds of gathering storm
Flame about my face and I cry out in alarm
   As I gather my cloak about me and turn to go.

Farther and farther I tread the unknown ways
My mind is swimming, my soul in a daze,
   The pain of the sword strikes through and through

And I sink to the ground bereft of sense
The pounding of my heart erects a fence
   Against what is unfaithful, old and untrue.

Oh, Ancient of Days, thou didst gyro and rave
At sacrifice of blood and all that I gave
   To children of earth from pelican's breast.

While the skies open up and the storm has burst
On pinion of thought and action that I durst,
   And love flows strangely into heart's nest.

1995

LOVE IS NOT A WORD

Love is not a word.
It is not even three words,
Spoken as, "I love you."
Love is a deed, an action
Because of a beautiful flower in the heart.
Do you love someone?
What do you do for those you love?
As a mother who loves her child
Is always alert to what is needed most;
Similarly, a person who loves others
Learns consideration and helpfulness,
Sympathy and empathy, a touching of hearts.
Love does not seek to own anyone else:
Love is not a projection
Of your own views and actions upon others.
Love does not judge nor complain
Because the loved ones do not behave
As you would behave or think.
Love forgives and forgets the mistakes
Of those beloved.
Love allows full freedom to BE to others:
In this, love does not fail or falter.
Love is not self-concern
It is an outreaching to the mystery
Shrouded in those unknown others.

If you would know the secret of pure love
It is the key to earthly and heavenly bliss.

1996

REINCARNATION[3]

As a phoenix arises from fire and ashes
So the end of life burns up in consuming flames
Until all that is left are the flashes
Of memory's accumulations laying claims

To all that went before in soul's growth.
Memories which can never be shaken
Out of the whole fabric of soul's cloth:
Memories until the soul demands to slaken

Thirst for life, for love at the fount of light.
So from life to life we end in heaven's fire
Doomed to struggle onward as best we might;
Our feet are not prisoned ever in earth's mire.

But respite comes upon us, though we forget
The rest and sweetness of death while on earth.
It is no use for ignorance to fret
About a new life, death means rebirth.

Ah, those we love, again we meet
Beyond the grave and in new lives too.
What use to mourn when in time we greet
Each other and live our lives anew.

---

[3] This poem was read at Soror Meral's memorial service in Sacramento, in June 2004, as she had requested.

But beware to hate for heaven's law
Decrees that karmic debts be paid.
And if a soul succumbs to such a flaw
Then many lives may pass before the error fades.

So now my loves, I depart upon my ways
And as the phoenix I will arise again
Out of the ashes of my numerous days
And we will dance to karmic strains.

We will learn to aspire always to the highest
Of aristocratic life, of refinement and love.
We will create again as does the artist
Whether of poesy, of painting, of music, until above:

We see our stars gleaming in heaven's dance:
We who are single sparks of fire in heaven's space.
Oh, set your sights on high, attain more than a glance
Of starlight bliss, of soul's greatest grace.

1996

ABOUT THE EDITORS

Dr. David Shoemaker is a clinical psychologist in private practice, specializing in Jungian and cognitive-behavioral psychotherapy. David is the Chancellor and Prolocutor of the Temple of the Silver Star. He is a long-standing member of O.T.O. and A∴A∴, and has many years of experience training initiates in these traditions.

He is the Master of 418 Lodge, O.T.O. in Sacramento, having succeeded Soror Meral (Phyllis Seckler), his friend and teacher. He also serves as the Most Wise Sovereign of Alpha Chapter, O.T.O., as a Sovereign Grand Inspector General and Bishop of Ecclesia Gnostica Catholica. David was the founding President of the O.T.O. Psychology Guild, and is a frequent speaker at national and regional conferences. He is also a member of the U.S. Grand Lodge Initiation Training and Planning committees, and he is a member of the Advanced Initiation Training presenter team.

David was a co-editor of the journals *Neshamah* (Psychology Guild) and *Cheth* (418 Lodge). In addition to his essays in these publications, his writings have been published in the journals *Mezlim* and *Black Pearl*, and his chapter on Qabalistic Psychology was included in the Instructor's Manual of Fadiman and Frager's *Personality and Personal Growth*, an undergraduate psychology textbook. He was the compiler of the T.O.T.S.S. publication, *Jane Wolfe: The Cefalu Diaries 1920-1923*, and a co-editor of the T.O.T.S.S./Teitan Press collections of the writings of Phyllis Seckler, *The Thoth Tarot, Astrology, & Other Selected Writings*, and *The Kabbalah, Magick, and Thelema. Selected Writings Volume II*. His popular *Living Thelema* instructional segments have been presented regularly on the podcast of the same name since 2010, and he is the author of the books *Living Thelema* and *The Winds of Wisdom*.

In addition to his work in magick and psychology, David is a composer and musician. He lives in Sacramento, California.

Lauren Gardner works as a counselor educator and psychotherapist. Her magical journey began nearly 20 years ago with an exploration into natural spirituality that evolved into ceremonial magick and ritual practice. In 2005, she was initiated into a local Golden Dawn temple, where she held key officer roles in initiations and Equinox ceremonies locally for nearly a decade. She contributed a chapter to Commentaries on the Golden Dawn Flying Rolls, published in 2013, and published several book reviews in Journal of the Western Mystery Tradition.

Currently, Lauren is actively involved with A∴A∴ including teaching and supervisory duties. She currently serves as EGC Coordinator at her local O.T.O. body, Star of Babalon Camp, in Raleigh, North Carolina. Lauren is a novice Priestess in the Gnostic Catholic Church. She was a presenter at O.T.O. Women's Symposium in 2016 and at NOTOCON XI in 2017.

In her professional life, Lauren is a therapist in part-time private practice and an educator involved in the training and supervision of mental health counselors. She particularly enjoys teaching psychological theories and is passionate about how knowledge of theory can spur students to a better understanding of themselves and those they serve. She has presented on the needs of the pagan population to her local professional organization, published in peer-reviewed journals, and presented at national counseling conferences. Lauren was a scholar of the American Academy of Psychotherapists in 2013.

Lauren lives with her cat in a quiet home in the forest near Raleigh, North Carolina.

Temple of the Silver Star - Academic Track

The Temple of the Silver Star is a non-profit religious and educational corporation, based on the principles of Thelema. It was founded in service to the A∴A∴, under warrant from Soror Meral (Phyllis Seckler), to provide preparatory training in magick, mysticism, Qabalah, Tarot, astrology, and much more. In its academic track, each student is assigned an individual teacher, who provides one-to-one instruction and group classes. Online classes and other distance-learning options are available.

The criteria for admission to the academic track of the Temple are explained on the application itself, which may be submitted online via the T.O.T.S.S. website. The Temple has campuses or study groups in Sacramento, Oakland, Los Angeles, Reno, Seattle, Denver, Boston, West Chester (Philadelphia-area), Toronto, Japan, Austria and the U.K. Public classes are offered regularly – schedules are available on our website.

Temple of the Silver Star - Initiatory Track

The Temple of the Silver Star's initiatory track offers ceremonial initiation, personalized instruction, and a complete system of training in the Thelemic Mysteries. Our degree system is based on the Qabalistic Tree of Life and the cipher formulæ of the Golden Dawn, of which we are a lineal descendant.

Our entire curriculum is constructed to be in conformity with the Law of Thelema, and our central aim is to guide each aspirant toward the realization of their purpose in life, or True Will. In order to empower our members to discover and carry out their True Will, we teach Qabalah, Tarot, ceremonial magick, meditation, astrology, and much more. Our initiates meet privately for group ceremonial and healing work, classes, and other instruction. We occasionally offer public classes and rituals.

Active participation in a local Temple or Pronaos is the best way to maximize the benefits of our system. However, we do offer At-Large memberships for those living at some distance from one of our local bodies.

If you are interested in learning more about our work, we invite you to download an application from our website and submit it to your nearest local body, or to contact us with any questions.

totss.org

Do what thou wilt shall be the whole of the Law.

The A∴A∴ is the system of spiritual attainment established by Aleister Crowley and George Cecil Jones in the early 1900s, as a modern expression of the Inner School of wisdom that has existed for millennia. Its central aim is simply to lead each aspirant toward their own individual attainment, for the betterment of all humanity. The course of study includes a diversity of training methods, such as Qabalah, raja yoga, ceremonial magick, and many other traditions. A∴A∴ is not organized into outer social organizations, fraternities or schools; rather, it is based on the time-tested power of individual teacher-student relationships, under the guidance of the masters of the Inner School. All training and testing is done strictly in accordance with *Liber 185* and other foundational documents.

Those interested in pursuing admission into A∴A∴ are invited to initiate contact via the following addresses:

A∴A∴
PO Box 215483
Sacramento, CA 95821
onestarinsight.org

The Student phase of preparation for work in A∴A∴ begins by acquiring a specific set of reference texts, notifying A∴A∴ of the same, and studying the texts for at least three months. The Student may then request Examination. More information about this process is available via the Cancellarius at the addresses given above. Please use only these contact addresses when initiating correspondence. While our primary contact address is in California, supervising Neophytes are available across the U.S. and in many countries around the world.

If you are called to begin this journey, we earnestly invite you to contact us. Regardless of your choice in this matter, we wish you the best as you pursue your own Great Work. May you attain your True Will!

Love is the law, love under will.

73688649R00077

Made in the
USA
Middletown, DE